MOUNTAINS

Franklin Watts

Published in paperback in Great Britain in 2018 by The Watts Publishing Group

Copyright © The Watts Publishing Group 2017

Produced for Franklin Watts by
White-Thomson Publishing Ltd
www.wtpub.co.uk
01273 479982

Series Editor: Izzi Howell
Series Designer: Rocket Design (East Anglia) Ltd

Alamy: Extreme Sports Photo 19b, Alan Gignoux 29b; iStock: bravobravo 7bl, jack0m 9bl, JTSorrell 11tl, jeremkin 15tl, andyKRAKOVSKI 15br, fotoVoyager 18b, JeffGoulden 22b, johnnya123 23t, sihasakprachum 26b, dibrova 27tc, Skouatroulio 27tb, viti 28c, dzubanovska 29t; Peter Bull 4-5, 19t, 20; Shutterstock: skelos 5t, 12t, 21l and 22t, fluidworkshop 6t, BlueRingMedia 7t, Arthur Balitskiy 7br, Matthijs Wetterauw 9tl, Darren J. Bradley 9tc, Chris Warham 9tr, Juergen Wackenhut 9br, Designua 10t, 10b, 11c and 17bl, iQoncept 10c, Krishna. Wu 11tr, Ecuadorpostales 13tl, Mossia 13b, Athanasia Nomikou 14, Francois Arseneault 15tr, Macrovector 15bl, chaoss 16tl, Venturelli Luca 16tr, Red monkey 16bl, corlaffra 17tr, URRRA 18t, Sopotnicki 21tr, Felix Lipov 21cr, StockPhotoAstur 21br, Sunny_nsk 23bl, Robert Biedermann 23cr, Tomacco 23br, Byelikova Oksana 24t, robuart 24b, Shirstok 25t, Seita 25b, Benjavisa Ruangvaree 26t, Daniel Prudek 27t, Sentavio 27bl, Allies Interactive 27br, Adazhiy Dmytro 28t, Krylovochka 28b; Techtype: 6b, 8t and 12b.

All design elements from Shutterstock: Meilun, Meowu, StockSmartStart, Blablo101, TyBy, GoodVector, DVARG, VectorShow, Oksana Alekseeva, SeneGal, Jane Kelly, polunoch and Iamnee.

ISBN 978 1 4451 5524 1

Printed in Dubai

MIX
Paper from
responsible sources
FSC® C104740
www.fsc.org

Franklin Watts
An imprint of
Hachette Children's Group
Part of The Watts Publishing Group
Carmelite House
50 Victoria Embankment
London EC4Y 0DZ

An Hachette UK Company
www.hachette.co.uk
www.franklinwatts.co.uk

Contents

What is a Mountain?

Mountains are high, rocky areas of land with steep, sloped sides. They are found on every continent on Earth. There are even mountains deep under the sea.

Mountains

There is no official minimum height for a mountain. However, most people would use the word 'mountain' to describe an area that rises dramatically higher than sea level and its surroundings. The bottom part of a mountain is called the base and the top is called the peak or summit.

peak

base
sea level

FOCUS ON **The Rocky Mountains (page 22)**

mountain ranges

FOCUS ON **The Appalachian Mountains (page 29)**

Mountain ranges

Mountains are millions of years old. The way in which mountains are created (see pages 8–11) means that they often form in groups, known as ranges. Well-known mountain ranges across the world include the Himalayas in Asia, the Alps in Europe, the Andes in South America and the Rocky Mountains in North America.

FOCUS ON **The Andes (page 12)**

Everest (8,848 m)
K2 (8,611 m)
Kangchenjunga (8,586 m)
Lhotse (8,516 m)
Makalu (8,485 m)

This map shows some of the main mountain ranges on Earth.

Record-breakers

While Everest is officially the highest mountain on Earth, there are many mountains that reach great heights.

 FOCUS ON **The Himalayas (page 26)**

There are also mountains on other planets. The tallest known mountain in our solar system is Olympus Mons on the planet Mars, which is 624 km wide and 25 km high. That's over three times the height of Everest!

FOCUS ON **The Alps (page 16)**

High and tall

There is a difference between the highest mountain and the tallest mountain on Earth. The highest mountain (measuring from sea level to peak) is Mount Everest, at 8,850 m. The tallest mountain (measuring from base to peak) is Mauna Kea, which is over 10,000 m tall. However, most of Mauna Kea is underwater, so it only measures 4,205 m from sea level.

Muving Plates

The Earth is made up of different layers of solid and liquid rock and metal. The movement of the outer layer creates mountains on the surface of the Earth.

The boundary between the inner and outer core can reach temperatures of 6,000 °C, which is as hot as the surface of the Sun!

Inside the Earth

There are four main layers inside the Earth. At the very centre is the inner core, which is made of solid iron. The outer core is a layer of liquid iron and nickel. The third layer is the mantle, which is composed of semi-molten rock (magma). The outermost layer or crust, is made of solid rock.

Crust – between 5 and 70 km thick ....

Mantle – 3,000 km thick ....

Outer core – 2,000 km thick ....

Inner core – 1,200 km thick ....

Plates

The Earth's crust is split into huge pieces of solid rock called tectonic plates. Continental plates lie under the continents and the land in shallow water along some coasts. Oceanic plates are found under the ocean. They are thinner but denser than continental plates. The area where plates meet is known as a boundary. Mountains, volcanoes and earthquakes are common at plate boundaries.

If you placed the east coast of South America and the west coast of Africa next to each other, they would roughly fit together. This is because they were once part of the same continent. Over millions of years, the continent split apart because of the movement of plates.

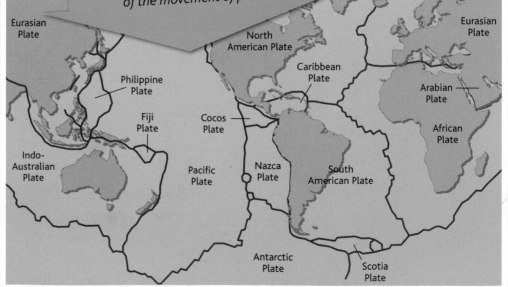

Eurasian Plate

Philippine Plate

Fiji Plate

Indo-Australian Plate

North American Plate

Caribbean Plate

Cocos Plate

Pacific Plate

Nazca Plate

South American Plate

Antarctic Plate

Scotia Plate

Eurasian Plate

Arabian Plate

African Plate

Convection currents

The high temperatures of the Earth's core heat magma in the mantle. This causes convection currents – movement in liquids caused by heat. The hot, semi-molten magma rises up while cool magma sinks towards the centre.

You can see convection currents when you heat water in a saucepan. The water closest to the heat source bubbles to the surface, while cooler water sinks down to the bottom.

Moving plates

The movement of the magma in the mantle makes the oceanic and continental plates slowly shift location. They travel a few centimetres every year. However, over millions of years, the movement of plates can make continents shift thousands of kilometres apart. This movement led to the separation of South America and Africa (see page 6).

plates moving away from each other

Types of movement

Plates move in three different ways. They can move towards each other, away from each other or slide past each other. The way in which plates move towards and away from each other creates mountains, volcanoes and earthquakes.

This canyon at the boundary between the Eurasian and North American plates in Iceland was formed by the plates moving away from each other.

plates moving towards each other

plates moving past each other

Fold and Block Mountains

Fold and block mountains are created when plates move towards each other. Some of the largest mountain ranges in the world, such as the Alps, the Himalayas and the Andes, are fold mountains.

Fold formation

When two plates move towards each other, the crust between them is pushed upwards. This tends to happen between continental plates. The compression of the crust makes it crease and fold. You can observe the same effect if you push the edges of a tablecloth together, creating ripples in the centre.

mountains are created

tectonic plate

tectonic plate

Folded ranges

At first, the crust is pushed into small folds. Over millions of years, the compression gets greater, and larger, deeper folds are created. This leads to the creation of large, dramatic mountain ranges, such as the Himalayas.

Microscopic fossilised seashells have been found near the summit of Everest. This is because the land at the peak of Everest was once underneath the ocean, before being pushed to its current height by tectonic forces.

Types of fold

We can observe different types of fold in the layers of rock that make up the Earth's crust. Most fold mountains have more than one type of fold. Curved, up and down folds are the most common. However, the layers can also be folded in a zig-zag shape or all slanted in one direction.

Some plates fold down when compression is applied, creating a U-shaped fold.

Upside-down, U-shaped folds are created when both sides of the rock are pushed inwards.

Zig-zag folds have straight folds with no curves.

Block mountains

When the Earth's crust breaks apart along a fault line, it forms several separate blocks of land. When tectonic forces push one block of land upwards and the blocks on either side downwards, it creates a block mountain.

These block mountains in the Black Forest, Germany, were pushed up along fault lines by tectonic forces. A small village has been built on the low, flat valley in between the mountains.

block mountain

block mountain

Volcanic Mountains

Many mountains around the world are or once were volcanoes. Volcanoes are places where hot magma from the mantle erupts through the surface of the Earth.

Underwater

Volcanoes are often created underwater when two oceanic plates move away from each other. Magma from the mantle rises up to fill the gap in between the plates.

plates moving away from each other

magma

Hotspots

Volcanoes also form in volcanic hotspots where the oceanic crust is very thin and easily melted by magma from the mantle. When the oceanic crust melts, more magma from the mantle breaks through, creating an underwater volcano that grows larger with each eruption.

The islands of Hawaii were created by volcanic hotspots in the Pacific Ocean. They are part of a chain of hundreds of islands, spread across 2,400 km.

Meeting plates

Volcanoes also occur along boundaries where oceanic and continental plates meet. When an oceanic plate collides with a continental plate, the denser oceanic plate is pushed underneath the continental plate. The oceanic plate is forced down into the mantle, where it melts into magma. This extra magma rises up to the surface of the continental plate, where it bursts out as a volcano.

continental plate

oceanic plate

mantle

magma

Types of volcano

Most people think of volcanoes as cone-shaped mountains. However, volcanoes can have many different shapes, depending on the amount and direction of lava flow.

Shield volcanoes are the largest type of volcano. They have gently sloping sides. They are formed by runny lava, which flows quickly across the land.

Mauna Kea in Hawaii is a shield volcano.

Stratovolcanoes have steep sides, formed from thick lava. The lava cannot flow far before it hardens, so it builds up on the side of the mountain.

Mount Fuji in Japan is a stratovolcano.

Extinct volcanoes

An extinct volcano will never erupt again. Scientists can predict if a volcano is extinct by measuring the amount of magma under the surface. If there is very little magma, the volcano is extinct. Some volcanoes are dormant, which means that it is unlikely, but not impossible, that they will erupt again.

There is a massive dormant volcano under the Yellowstone National Park (USA). It hasn't erupted for 630,000 years but if it erupts again, it will affect the climate around the world and its lava will cover a huge area of land!

FOCUS ON The Andes

The Andes are the longest mountain range on Earth. They stretch along the west coast of South America, from tropical Venezuela in the north to icy Patagonia in the south.

Plate collision

The Andes were created millions of years ago, when the South American continental plate collided with the Nazca and Antarctic oceanic plates. The continental plate was pushed over the denser oceanic plate. This created many volcanic mountains.

80 to 100 mm of the Nazca plate is disappearing under the South American plate every year.

0 mm   100 mm

actual size

GUYANA
SURINAME
FRENCH GUIANA
VENEZUELA
COLOMBIA
Quito
Chimborazo
Equator
EQUADOR
Andes
PERU
BRAZIL
Lake Titicaca
BOLIVIA
Altiplano
PARAGUAY
Mount Aconcagua
CHILE
Ojos
del
Salado
Andes
URUGUAY
Pacific Ocean
ARGENTINA
Atlantic Ocean
Patagonia

Volcanic mountains

Most mountains along the Andes are volcanoes. Some of them have been extinct or dormant for many years. Others still erupt frequently. The world's highest active volcano, Ojos del Salado, which stands at 6,893 m, is located in the Andes.

The eruption of the Cotopaxi volcano in the Andes in 2015 was visible 50 km away in Quito, the capital of Ecuador.

Altiplano

As well as steep mountains, there are high plateaus in the Andes, such as the Altiplano. The Altiplano is a flat, dry area in Bolivia and Peru that reaches around 3,800 m above sea level. It was created very quickly, when tectonic forces lifted up an area of the crust.

Chimborazo is a dormant volcano in the Andes, near to the equator in Ecuador. Because the Earth bulges at the equator, the peak of Chimborazo is actually further from the centre of the Earth than the peak of Mount Everest.

Mount Aconcagua

Not all mountains in the Andes are volcanoes. Mount Aconcagua, the highest mountain in the Andes and the highest mountain outside of Asia, is a fold mountain. However, Mount Aconcagua was also created by the same event that made the volcanoes along the Andes – the collision of the South American and the Nazca plate.

Basins

There are several basins across the Altiplano. Lake Titicaca, the world's highest navigable lake, is located in a basin in the north of the plateau. In the south of the Altiplano, water has evaporated from basins that were once prehistoric lakes, leaving behind large flat areas covered in a thick crust of salt and minerals.

Changing Mountains

Mountains are always changing shape. Erosion and landslides cause parts of their rocky slopes to fall and wear away, giving them their characteristic jagged shape. Glaciers also carve deep valleys through mountainous areas.

Rock

The type of rock that a mountain is made from affects the speed at which it erodes. Areas of soft rock will erode more quickly than areas of hard rock.

In the past, the Appalachian Mountains were taller than the Himalayas, but after millions of years of erosion, they are now thousands of metres shorter.

Water

Rain, rivers and other forms of moving water can dramatically erode rock. Rain gets into cracks on the mountain slopes, breaking away chunks of rock. Rainwater that is not absorbed by the ground also flows down the side of the mountain, carrying particles of soil and small rocks with it. Most rivers begin in high, mountainous ground. They flow quickly downhill from their source, carving channels and valleys into the slopes.

Wind

Mountains are very windy as there is nothing to block the wind at such great heights. Strong winds erode mountains by blowing away loose rock. Tiny pieces of rock are picked up by the wind and blown against the mountainside, wearing the slope away further.

Temperature changes

Rising and falling temperatures affect erosion. When the temperature drops below 0°C, any water that has fallen between rocks or been absorbed by the soil freezes solid. The frozen water expands, creating cracks in the rock and soil. When the temperature rises and the ice melts, these loose chunks of rock and soil fall away easily.

Glaciers

Slow moving rivers of ice, known as glaciers, are often found in high mountain ranges. The weight and force of the ice, combined with rocks suspended in the glacier, cuts through the land, creating U-shaped valleys at the base of mountains. In the past, the Earth's climate was much colder and there were many more glaciers than nowadays. These glaciers, which have since melted, cut out valleys that can still be seen today.

Landslides

Gravity will eventually pull any unsupported rock or mud down the side of a mountain. Heavy rains or strong winds can loosen large amounts of rock and mud. This material can fall all at once, as part of a landslide. The force and weight of the falling rock erodes the lower slopes as it makes its way down.

In this landslide, fallen rock from the peak of the mountain has nearly reached the base.

Caves

Some mountains have deep caves hidden inside them. These caves are usually carved out of the rock by water, which is absorbed through the ground and slowly wears away large, hollow underground spaces.

This cave inside a volcano was formed by magma. When a volcano becomes dormant, the tubes that the magma once flowed through are left empty.

FOCUS ON — The Alps

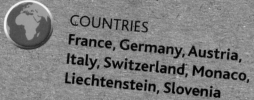

LENGTH
1,200 km

HIGHEST POINT
4,810 m
(Mont Blanc)

COUNTRIES
France, Germany, Austria, Italy, Switzerland, Monaco, Liechtenstein, Slovenia

The Alps are a crescent-shaped mountain range in southern Europe. They are the biggest mountain range in Europe, stretching through eight countries.

Formation

The Alps are fold mountains. They were created when the African tectonic plate moved towards the Eurasian plate, pushing up the land in between into high mountain peaks. The same movement also formed the Pyrenees – a range of mountains on the border between France and Spain.

The peak of Mont Blanc is covered with a dome of ice in winter. This means that the mountain can measure up to 16 m higher in winter than in summer.

The Matterhorn

Originally, the Matterhorn mountain in the Alps had a rounded shape, like a hill. However, in summer, the ice that covers the high peak of the mountain melts and falls into cracks in the rock. In winter, the water freezes, fracturing the rock, which then falls off. Over millions of years, this cycle of erosion has changed the shape of the mountain from hill to pyramid.

Glaciers of the past

The Alps were home to many glaciers thousands of years ago, when the Earth had a much colder climate. As the temperature increased over time, these glaciers melted, creating rivers and leaving behind large piles of rocks. However, some glaciers still exist in the Alps.

Disappearing glaciers

As the Earth's temperature continues to increase due to climate change, the remaining glaciers in the Alps are in danger of disappearing. The melting of these glaciers could cause flooding so scientists are trying to find ways to slow it down. One effective method is to put huge sheets over the glaciers in summer, which stop the Sun's rays from hitting the ice and keep it cool.

Causing an avalanche

Avalanches often happen after heavy snowfall. The weight of the heavy extra snow is so great that it slides down the mountain. As it falls, it picks up more snow, ice and rocks from further down the mountain. Earthquakes regularly start avalanches. They can also be triggered by human activity, such as the vibrations caused by noise, skiing and helicopters.

heavy extra snow

snowfall

sliding snow

Avalanches

An avalanche is a large amount of snow, ice and rock that suddenly falls down a mountain. They are common in the Alps. Avalanches are one of the most dangerous and destructive events that can happen on a mountain. The weight and force of the falling snow can kill people and damage forests and buildings on its way down.

This photo shows an avalanche in the Alps. Snow from near the peak of this mountain has slid downhill towards the base, leaving the bare rock exposed.

Deadly snow

In the winter of 1950-1, there were nearly 650 avalanches in the Alps, due to unusually heavy snow. This period is known as the Winter of Terror. Over 250 people were killed in just three months. The avalanches destroyed many villages and areas of forest. In recent years, early warning systems have been installed. They send out an alarm if an avalanche is coming, which gives people some time to evacuate.

90% of people who die in avalanches caused the avalanche themselves.

Climate

The climate at high altitudes is different to the weather conditions in low areas. The higher the altitude, the colder and windier the weather.

Mountain peaks

The top part of most mountains sticks up high above the surrounding landscape. There is nothing of a similar height nearby to block strong winds or to trap warm air. This is why mountain peaks are extremely windy and cold. The light at high altitudes is also very intense, as the Sun's rays reflect off the snow.

Seasons

At the top of a mountain, the weather is cold all year round. The ice and snow at the peak may never melt. Lower down the mountain, there is more variety between the seasons. Winters are still cold, but there can be warm weather in the summer.

The snow at the peaks of the Himalayas never melts. Towards the base of the mountains, the climate is warmer and small plants can grow.

Shadows

Some parts of a mountain are always in shadow, as the high peak of the mountain blocks light from the Sun. This makes them much cooler than areas that receive sunlight. High mountain peaks can also create a rain shadow effect, as they block rain-carrying clouds.

The air cools near the mountains and clouds form.

When warm, moist air comes on to land from the ocean, it is carried inland by the wind towards mountains.

Most of the rain from the clouds falls on the slope of the mountain that faces the sea.

Less rain falls on the other side of the mountain. This area is in a rain shadow.

Oxygen

There is less oxygen in the air at high altitude. Humans and animals need oxygen to survive. If there is less oxygen available, their bodies need to work harder than usual to keep healthy. This can make people feel ill and can even cause death (see page 24).

Death zone

Above 8,000 m, there is not enough oxygen in the air for humans or most animals to survive. This area is known as the death zone. Cranes and whooper swans are among the few species of animal that can survive in the death zone.

The summit of Mount Everest is in the death zone. People who climb to high altitudes on Everest breathe oxygen from tanks through masks.

Biomes

The landscape, climate, animals and plants on a mountain change greatly depending on the altitude. There are many different biomes across mountainous areas.

Biome height

At the base of a mountain, there is often flat grassland or savannah. On the lower slopes, there are temperate forests made up of deciduous trees. Higher up, there is taiga forest with mainly evergreen trees. At around 3,000 m above sea level, the landscape changes to alpine tundra. The highest mountains have no plants at the top, just frozen ice and snow.

Ice

Tundra: low plants, mosses and lichens

Taiga: evergreen trees, which stay green all year round

Temperate forest: deciduous trees, which lose their leaves in autumn

Grassland: scattered trees and grasses

Treeline

The boundary between taiga forest and tundra is known as the treeline. This is the highest point at which trees can grow. Above this line, the temperatures are too low for trees to grow. Trees also can't get enough moisture from the soil, as any water is frozen into ice or snow.

Landscape

Near the base, mountains usually have gentle slopes, covered with soil and plants. Higher up, there are more areas of jagged, exposed rock with some steep cliffs. It is much harder for animals and humans to climb over this rocky terrain. However, some mountain herbivores, such as goats, are able to jump from rock to rock. They stay safe from predators by climbing steep slopes that other animals can't reach.

Animal and plant adaptations

Mountain animals have adapted to move around easily on the slopes. They need to be agile with a good sense of balance. Plants have developed ways to protect themselves from the extreme conditions, such as growing hairs on their leaves to block intense sunlight. Many plants also grow low to the ground to avoid the strong winds.

The chamois has flexible hooves that help them to scramble up rocky slopes.

The bristlecone pine grows incredibly slowly to conserve energy, as there are few nutrients in the rocky mountain soil.

The griffon vulture has good eyesight to spot dead animals lying on the mountainside, while it is soaring high above.

Extreme conditions

There are many dangers for humans on mountains. There is a risk of landslides and avalanches, falling from a sheer drop or problems from being exposed to freezing, windy conditions. However, these risks can benefit mountain animals, as it means that their habitats are mainly untouched by human activity.

! Some insects manage to survive at great heights. There are bumblebees and spiders that live above 5,500 m on Mount Everest. The spiders eat insects that have been carried up the mountainside by wind.

FOCUS ON The Rocky Mountains

The Rocky Mountains stretch inland along the west coast of North America. A wide range of animals and plants live in the biomes found at different altitudes.

FACT FILE

 LENGTH
4,800 km

 HIGHEST POINT
4,401 m (Mount Elbert)

 COUNTRIES
Canada and the USA

Forests

As with many mountain ranges, the lower slopes of the Rocky Mountains are covered in temperate forests, with taiga higher up. There is no clear division between the two. The forests naturally blend together as the altitude increases.

Twisted trees

Many of the trees at the very edge of the treeline in the Rocky Mountains grow in stunted, twisted shapes. This is because the very strong, icy winds kill branches in their path. Other parts of the tree grow in different directions to avoid the wind.

Twisted trees that grow high on mountains are also known as krummholz trees. Krummholz means bent wood in German.

Grassland

The bottom of valleys and slopes in the Rocky Mountains are covered in grassland. There are also large areas of grassland to the east of the Rocky Mountains, known as the Great Plains.

Alpine tundra

Grasses and wildflowers grow in the alpine tundra above the treeline in the Rocky Mountains. In spring, the flowering plants brings colour to the slopes. As the altitude increases, the number of plants decreases. The peaks of the Rocky Mountains are just exposed rock.

In this section of the Rocky Mountains in Utah, the layers of ice, tundra and forest are clearly visible.

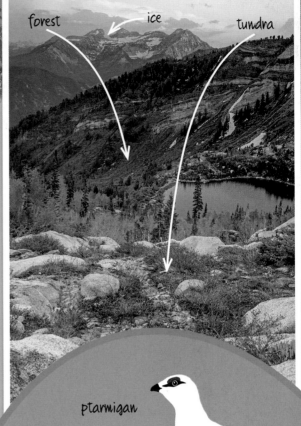

forest   ice   tundra

Predators

Large numbers of black bears live in remote forests across the Rocky Mountains. They mainly eat plants, but they will also hunt young deer and mountain goats. The grey wolf population is growing. Having a high number of grey wolves helps to keep the forest biome in balance, as the wolves' diet of elk and deer keeps the number of plant-eating animals from getting too high.

Sheep, deer and elk

Elk and deer mainly live in the temperate forests and taiga, feeding on leaves and berries. Bighorn sheep (below) are agile enough to climb up to the alpine meadows. They graze on grass and can live in relative peace, away from forest predators.

ptarmigan

Birds

Birds of prey, such as owls and eagles, hunt in the forests and exposed rocky slopes of the Rocky Mountains. Above the tree line, ptarmigans feed on plants in the tundra. Ptarmigans grow white feathers in winter for camouflage against the snow.

! The Rocky Mountains are home to the bald eagle, the national animal of the USA. In the past, the bald eagle population dropped dramatically due to hunting and deaths from pesticides. Recently, protection programmes have helped the number of birds in the mountains to recover.

People and Mountains

At least 140 million people around the world have made their homes at or above 2,400 m above sea level. They have learned how to adapt to life on the inhospitable mountain slopes.

Towns

Conditions in small towns on high mountain ranges can be tough. Food and other supplies can be hard to come by. The towns often lack sewage systems and running water because people can't transport machines to construct these systems up the mountain. If people suffer medical emergencies, they are far from medical assistance and hospitals.

La Paz in Bolivia is the highest city in the world. Some parts of the city are very hard to access by car, so they have installed a public cable car system.

Living at altitude

People who live at high altitudes have to adjust to life with much less oxygen. Receiving less oxygen than usual can make people feel dizzy and out of breath and can give them headaches and stomach problems. However, this is more of a problem for visitors to high altitudes than for people who have lived at high altitude for many generations. Scientists have observed that the bodies of these people have adapted so that they are less affected by altitude sickness.

The highest permanent settlement in the world is La Rinconada in Peru, which sits at 5,100 m above sea level. Most of the town's 50,000 inhabitants were attracted to the town between 2001 and 2009 by jobs in the local gold mine.

Mountain activities

Many people travel to the mountains for holidays. Winter sports such as skiing and snowboarding attract many visitors to the slopes every year. All-year-round activities such as hiking and rock climbing are also popular.

Exploring mountains

In the 19th century, Western explorers began to try to reach the peaks of mountains around the world. The most challenging mountains to climb were the Himalayas and in particular, Mount Everest. Many famous climbers lost their lives trying to reach the summit of Everest. Finally, in 1953, Sir Edmund Hillary and Tenzing Norgay made it to the top. There are still hundreds of unconquered mountains around the world, such as the 7,570-m-high Gangkhar Puensum in Bhutan.

Food

It is hard to grow food on steep mountain slopes. There is little flat land for farming and the rocky soil isn't very fertile. Only certain crops, such as rice, will grow in the extreme weather conditions.

! The boiling point of water gets lower as the altitude increases. This makes it harder to cook foods in water, as boiling water isn't as hot as it is at sea level!

Travelling up mountains

For some people, mountain climbing is a hobby, but for others, it's the only way for them to move around. It is hard to build roads and railways up mountain slopes, so people are forced to travel on foot. They use animals such as llamas, donkeys and yaks to carry heavy loads.

Threats

High numbers of visitors threaten some fragile mountain regions. When people walk along and around mountain trails, they often drop litter, damage plants and wear away rocks, increasing the risk of landslides. By making mountains into national parks, we can control the number of visitors and protect the habitat from future damage.

The Himalayas

The Himalayan mountain range is home to some of the highest mountains in the world. Despite the high altitude, there are many small towns scattered across the Himalayas.

Lifestyle

Many people in the Himalayas work as farmers, raising livestock or growing crops. The facilities in their towns are very basic and people have little access to running water, electricity and sewage systems.

FACT FILE

LENGTH
2,500 km

HIGHEST POINT
8,850 m (Mount Everest)

COUNTRIES
Bhutan, India, Nepal, China, Pakistan, Afghanistan

Tourism

There are advantages and disadvantages to tourism in the Himalayas. People can earn extra income by providing food and rooms for tourists or by selling guided tours and souvenirs. However, large groups of tourists put pressure on the town's facilities, leaving less electricity and clean water for the local community.

Getting around

There are few road networks high in the Himalayas. People have to carry food, medicine and building supplies up the sides of the mountains. They use yaks to carry the heaviest objects and transport the rest on their own backs. Some children have to walk and climb for many hours to get to school every day. A few children are sent to boarding school to avoid this problem.

Sherpas

People from the Sherpa ethnic group live in Nepal. They are expert mountaineers and are well known for their work as guides, assisting people who want to climb the Himalayas. The best-known Sherpa is Tenzing Norgay, who reached the top of Mount Everest in 1953, accompanied by Sir Edmund Hillary (see page 25).

These Sherpa men are carrying expedition kit up to Everest Base Camp.

Mountain towns

Most people in the Himalayas live in small villages. However, there are also growing towns and cities. Some have been around for centuries, while others have grown larger because of tourism.

NAMCHE BAZAAR – 3,440 m *This village and trading hub is located in the Nepalese section of the Himalayas. It is a popular stop-off point for climbers who are heading to the base camp on Mount Everest. They often stay for several days so that their bodies can adjust to the high altitude.*

LHASA – 3,650 m *220,000 people live in the city of Lhasa in the Tibet Autonomous Region of China. It is one of the highest cities in the world and is filled with Buddhist temples and shrines, which attract many visitors. It is fairly easy to reach Lhasa, as it is connected to other settlements by roads, railways and airlines.*

LEH – 3,500 m *In the past, the town of Leh in India was an important trade centre. It was in the middle of trading routes between the east and the west, so many traders passed through looking for food and shelter. The town is near the fertile Indus Valley, so it is easier for people to come by a variety of foods.*

OM MA NI PADME HUM

prayer flags

Religion

In the north of the Himalayas, most people are Buddhist. They build shrines and temples high in the mountains. Buddhists often hang colourful prayer flags high on mountain slopes, which they believe will bless the area. Towards the south, most people follow the Hindu religion.

Food and drink

Grains, such as buckwheat, barley and millet, are some of the few foods that grow in the harsh climate of the Himalayas. These grains are ground into flour, which is used to make noodles and dumplings. People drink butter tea, often made with yak's milk butter. This tea is high in calories, which people need to survive the cold weather.

dumplings

butter tea

Mountain Resources

Useful resources, such as rocks and trees, can be gathered from mountain slopes. People dig inside mountains to mine precious rocks and stones, which can be sold at a high price.

Building materials

Mountain slopes are often made from rocks that we often use in construction, such as marble, limestone and granite. Large blocks of these rocks are cut away from the slopes in quarries. Later, they are cut down into smaller pieces and used as flooring and wall coverings, and to make sculptures.

Mining

Some resources are found deep inside mountains. Miners dig down and use explosive materials to create mines, where copper, gold and other metals can be extracted. Mining can make mountains unstable, as the tunnels may not be able to support the weight of the rock above. This can result in the collapse of some areas of the mountain.

Large amounts of the marble on the slopes of these Italian mountains has been cut away.

FOCUS ON

The Appalachian Mountains

The Appalachian Mountains are a mountain range in the east of North America. They are relatively low mountains that are rich in natural resources, such as coal and oil.

FACT FILE

LENGTH
3,200 km

HIGHEST POINT
2,037 m (Mount Mitchell)

COUNTRIES
Canada, USA

History

In the past, people mined coal using pick-axes and explosives in underground mines in the Appalachian Mountains. This was dangerous, as it was hard to control the explosions. It took a large number of workers a long time to extract the coal.

Mountaintop removal

In the 1960s, people started using explosives to remove the tops of mountains. This left the coal inside the mountain exposed, so it could be easily cut away. The benefit of this was that fewer workers could extract more coal in safer conditions.

This photo shows the effects of mountaintop removal mining in the Appalachian Mountains.

Damage

Mountaintop removal mining has had a negative effect on the environment in the Appalachian Mountains. Many animals have lost their habitats as the trees on the slopes were removed before the mountaintop removal mining and weren't replanted afterwards. Piles of rock from the mountaintops have been abandoned in nearby valleys. The mining has also affected the water supply in the area, as several rivers that began in the mountains have lost their sources. Dangerous chemicals and waste from the mines have poisoned the water and the land.

DANGER!

Glossary

altitude height above sea level

altitude sickness breathing problems and dizziness caused by not having enough oxygen due to high altitude

avalanche a large amount of snow, rock and ice that falls down the side of a mountain

biomes natural areas on Earth that have the same climate, landscape, plants and animals

boarding school a school where students live and study

compression pressing something into a smaller space

continental plate a large piece of the Earth's crust that lies under a continent and along some coasts

convection current movement caused by hot liquid rising and cool liquid falling

core the centre of the Earth

crust the outer layer of the Earth

deciduous describes trees that lose their leaves in autumn and regrow their leaves in spring

dense the molecules in a dense substance are closely compacted together

dormant a dormant volcano is unlikely to erupt soon

erosion the process in which water and wind gradually wear away rock and soil

evergreen describes trees that have leaves that stay green all year

extinct an extinct volcano will never erupt again

fertile describes land where plants can grow well

glacier a large amount of ice that moves slowly

grassland a biome that is mainly covered in grass plants with few trees

landslide the movement of rocks and earth down a steep slope

lava hot, melted rock outside a volcano

magma hot, melted rock inside a volcano

mantle the layer of the Earth underneath the crust

navigable describes an area of water deep enough to sail a boat on

oceanic plate a large piece of the Earth's crust that lies under the ocean

peak the top point of a mountain

plate boundary the place where two tectonic plates meet

plateau a large, flat, high area

sea level the height of the sea where it meets the land

settlement a place where humans have settled and live permanently, such as a town

source the place where a river starts

taiga a forest biome with mainly evergreen trees

tectonic plate a section of the Earth's crust

treeline the maximum height where trees will grow on a mountain

tundra a cold biome with few plants that is covered by ice for most of the year

Test yourself!

1 How tall is Olympus Mons, the largest known mountain in our solar system?

2 What is the Earth's crust made from?

3 What is a dormant volcano?

4 Name two things that trigger avalanches.

5 Which biome is usually found above taiga on mountainsides?

6 Who were the first people to reach the summit of Mount Everest?

7 Why is it hard to cook food at high altitudes?

8 Name two countries that the Himalayas pass through.

! *Check your answers on page 32.*

Further reading

At Home in the Biome: Mountains
Louise and Richard Spilsbury (Wayland, 2016)

Climbing the Himalayan Mountains
Sonya Newland (Wayland, 2016)

Geographywise: Mountains
Jen Green (Wayland, 2014)

Websites

Read more about mountains at the following websites:

www.dkfindout.com/uk/earth/mountains/

www.ducksters.com/science/earth_science/mountain_geology.php

www.bbc.co.uk/nature/habitats/Mountain

Index

Answers

1 25 km

2 Solid rock

3 A volcano that is unlikely to erupt again.

4 Some examples include earthquakes, heavy snowfall and vibrations from human activity.

5 Tundra

6 Sir Edmund Hillary and Tenzing Norgay

7 Because the boiling point of water gets lower as the altitude increases, so boiling water isn't as hot as it is at sea level.

8 Bhutan, India, Nepal, China, Pakistan or Afghanistan